T0065240

CRYING HEART

CRYING
HEART

L. ROSE

CRYING HEART

iUniverse books may be ordered through booksellers or by contacting:

iUniverse
1663 Liberty Drive
Bloomington, IN 47403
www.iuniverse.com
844-349-9409

ISBN: 978-1-6632-1286-3 (sc)
ISBN: 978-1-6632-1345-7 (e)

Print information available on the last page.

iUniverse rev. date: 11/18/2020

MEMORIES OF MY childhood I can never forget, from a young age. I was about six years old, as I can recall the abuse. I never forget.

I was living with my stepmother and my father, who was separated from my mom. My natural mother wanted to raise me, but my father would not let her. My mom and dad, my grandma, and my aunt – we all lived together. They all were raising me at one time until my mom and dad were not getting along anymore, when my dad started to stay out, not coming home. He was starting to have other girlfriends.

We all lived in Brooklyn, New York. My mom did not know her way around too much. She was from Puerto Rico. She was looking for a job, and she got one, so that she could help out with the bills.

My aunt was not happy. She never liked my mother. They could not get along at all.

My dad was always working. He has been working since he was thirteen years old. He went to school through the third or fourth grade, and they were very poor. He also was from Puerto Rico.

My dad and mom met in Puerto Rico. They got married, and they moved to New York. I was born in New York. I have never been to Puerto Rico.

Anyway, at six years old I remember my dad taking me away from my mom. He left my mom and said I had a new stepmom. I was not happy. I knew I was leaving my mom. What could I do? All I did was cry, and my mom was sad and upset too.

We left and went to see my stepmom, who also lived in Brooklyn. We got there, and my dad knocked on her door. She opened it, said hi to me. I looked at her, and we went in.

I saw a girl my age, and she was pretty. We all were talking, but I felt really hurt because I would not see my home. My dad brought my clothes up to her house, and I was still upset and hurt, though everything seemed nice and happy there.

After that day it was hard. The second and third day I was starting to get used to being there and not with my mom.

My dad was working, and I did not get to talk to him much. He worked hard. I saw him about three-thirty p.m. when he got off work. He would be tired from working, and sometimes he worked overtime, so that when he would come home, we would already be asleep.

Well, I started school – new faces, new kids. It was okay. I liked school, but I was upset knowing my mom was not with me.

My stepsister was a little nice. It seemed as though she did not like me much. She knew that I was not her real sister.

I asked my dad, "How about me going to visit my mom and grandma?"

He said, "Yeah, on weekends."

I was real happy for that. I couldn't wait to go. I was so anxious, so happy.

The next week came. I didn't see my dad much. He got off work late, and by that time I was asleep.

The next morning I was sad. By the time I got up, he was already gone.

Maybe I will see him after school, if he gets off work early today.

My dad was becoming a stranger to me. When I got to see him, I asked him if he could take me out to my mom's or grandma's, and he said, "Okay, next weekend."

Again I had to wait. I was upset.

As days went by, my stepmom wanted me to clean more and had more chores for me to do. I did not mind. I did them. At the same time I was upset and started to be unhappy.

I also noticed I did not go out much. I went from school home, home to the store, or did not go out at all. That was making me too sad.

Weeks were still going by, and no Mom, no Grandma. I didn't see anybody. It was just school, home, and the store. I was starting to be hurt, really hurt.

My stepmom was putting me to bed earlier now, and I had to follow rules. I didn't' like it.

My stepmom was having a baby. Everybody was happy but me. I was sad, and becoming more sad every day. My dad was happy. He acted as though I was not around the house.

My stepsister said very little to me. She started saying I was just a stepsister around here, that's all.

Now I was really sad. I did not say anything to anyone. I was afraid.

I also noticed my stepsister was getting more things than I was. She would get more clothes than me, shoes and all. She had her own bedroom.

Days and weeks went by. The baby was born. It was a girl. Everybody was happy except me. My dad would not say much to me at all.

What's going to happen to me? I wondered.

I wanted to see my mom, my grandma, or my aunt, because I knew they loved me. I was eight years old and still doing the same thing. I never got to see my mom or grandma. I felt lost from my family.

It's my dad's fault. He took me away from my mom, to come and live here.

My stepmom had another baby, another step sister.

I was doing good in school except for math. I did not keep my mind on math.

A year went by, and it was the same thing. I never got to visit anyone. It was just school, chores, and the store. I couldn't even visit a friend. I was just afraid of what would happen to me.

I went to school one day and had a nice day until three o'clock, when some girls were making fun of me and pulling my hair. I cried and ran home. After I got home, I did not say anything to anyone about what happened to me after school.

I had a lot of homework, and I never had anyone to help me do it, not even my dad. He had no time for me. My stepmom was becoming very bossy with me. She wanted me to do a lot of chores, and I felt she gave me too many chores to do. I did them but was not happy.

Anyway, my stepmom was having another baby, but I wasn't happy. When it was time to go to school, I wasn't happy. I just felt I just did not care anymore.

It was time for me to come home one day, and I came late, walking slow, talking to some friends on my way. As soon as I stepped into the house, she grabbed me and said I was late. She hit me, then beat me up.

I was screaming loud so everyone could hear me, crying and screaming.

My stepmom said, "I'm telling your dad. He's going to beat you."

I was really afraid. I went in my room, and I didn't want to come out. I had to come out to do my chores though – throw out the trash, go to the store – and I did it but was not happy.

My dad came home, and she told him I was late from school. He got upset and called me by my nickname, though everyone else called me by my name. He asked me why I was late, and I did not say anything, so he hit me also.

I was crying loud when I went in my room. I was upset, mad, and starting to feel hatred.

It was time to eat supper, and I felt I could not eat, being so upset and nervous at the same time. I ate some, then took a bath and went to sleep. I was so upset, I cried myself to sleep.

The next day it was time to get up and go to school, and she woke me up real early.

For what? I wondered. *Am I leaving here to see my mom?*

I got dressed quickly and had a little breakfast. It was six-thirty in the morning, and she told me to do the wash at the laundromat. I looked at her and left. The laundry placed opened at six in the morning – and that was not all. I had to clean and do chores before I left for school.

After I did everything, I had to go to school late. I did not like that. I was embarrassed.

I said to myself, *I have to do this every day. I will never make it. It's impossible.*

My dad had no time for me.

What's happening to me? Why me? Why me?

I felt this way every day. I didn't care anymore. It seemed to grow more and more, my not caring about anyone. That's how I felt every single day. There was not a day when I felt right about myself.

It was Saturday. Maybe I could get a chance to ask my dad to take me away to see my mom, my aunt, somebody, but away from here. It was the only thing I knew – my stepmom's chores. I was so sick of it, I could not stand it.

I finally saw my dad, so I could ask, "Can I go see my family?"

The answer was no. That broke my heart. I broke out in tears and walked away, real sad.

A few years went by, and I was doing the same thing, every morning, every day. I started to come home from school late every day, and I got beatings every day. I did it on purpose. I did not care.

I was used to it already, beatings from my stepmom, then my dad. She started to lie about me, telling my dad things about me that were not true.

I kept living like that, year after year. Now I was about eleven years old, and it was still the same old thing. Getting older, I was skinny. I knew one day I would have freedom, somehow, some way.

I will! One day I'll see my mom again...one day...one day....

My dad came home late from work, and I noticed my stepmom, seemed upset. I did not know why. Finally my dad came home, and she was upset that he came home too late. They were arguing, and I was happy.

She was screaming. He got louder. I was smiling.

I was hurting bad, but he did not know what was going on with me, the things my stepmom had me do, the chores I had to do, the beatings I got from her after school. Then my dad would get off work.

Again I was going to wait for the weekend to ask my dad to take me to see my family. The arguing was over.

The next day, it was school and chores, as usual, including washing and getting the newspaper. At that time the newspaper was ten cents. I went to the newspaper stand to buy the paper, and there were so many people there grabbing newspapers that I got one and kept going, keeping the dime. I got candy. It was the only time I had any kind of money.

I started doing that. I kept doing it every single day, like always going late to school. It was the same old thing, and one thing I never told anyone about, not my teachers, no one. I was too afraid.

Friday is here already. I am going to ask my dad to take me to my family.

School was over, and I was waiting for my dad to come home from work.

He came, and I had a chance to ask, "Please take me to my family."

He said yes. Finally he said yes!

I was so happy, my heart was beating so fast, I could have screamed.

He said, "Get ready. We are going later."

Oh, my God! I was so happy! *Oh! Oh!*

My stepsister gave me an ugly look. I was so happy, I couldn't wait.

I must tell someone what has been happening to me all this time. Maybe someone can help me get out of this place.

I was getting dressed. My clothes were in a bag. I was ready to leave in my dad's car. I was waiting around, waiting to leave.

I said to myself, *This is my big chance to spill out everything that has been done to me.*

It was time to go, and we left. As we got in the car, I felt beautiful, so free, so happy to get away from there. It was a good feeling. I was happy but still scared.

It's only a weekend. I have to come back.

Still I was happy. My dad and I didn't say much along the way. He had the radio on, and he would smile at me.

We arrived at my aunt's house, and we got out of the car and knocked at my aunt's door. I was really happy.

I wonder if she looks the same. Did she change?

They opened the door, and it was my aunt and uncle and cousin. Wow! We stepped in, and everybody said hello, but I was a little shy.

We drank some soda, and my uncle offered my dad a beer. They were talking.

My aunt said, "You are big – and pretty." Then she asked, "What's the matter?"

I told her, "I am not happy. I'll tell you everything when my dad leaves."

She looked at me, very worried.

My aunt told all the kids to go outside. I looked at my cousin, and she said yes and went outside.

Her name was Millie.

"I said go outside and play!" she screamed.

I told my aunt, "Me too?"

She said, "Yes, go outside with Millie."

This was what I called happiness, fun, beautiful. It was beautiful! We went outside. It was about six o'clock. We jumped rope, and when the ice-cream truck went by, my aunt gave us all money.

Ice cream – and freedom!

Boy, I didn't know how to act. I forgot about my stepmom.

My dad was getting ready to leave, and he told me, "Be ready on Sunday. I'll come pick you up."

He kissed me, and then he left.

My aunt said, "Leave her some money, so she can buy things," and he did.

Money for me to spend! Wow!

My dad left, and my aunt called me to her bedroom.

I asked her, "Where is my mom?"

She said, "I don't know where she lives. We all separated when you left."

I told her about my stepmom, little by little. I told her I did not want to be there anymore.

She said, "Oh, my God!" and shook her head. "Does your dad know about your stepmom?"

I said, "No. I get beatings from her, and then from my dad also. He believes her, everything she tells him. He believes her!"

She said, "I'll take you to your grandma's tomorrow."

My eyes got big. Grandma! I was really happy.

She sent us in to take a bath. Then it was snacks, TV, and bed at ten o'clock.

I told her, "I never felt so happy."

My aunt said, "I can imagine what you have been going through. Why doesn't your father know?"

I told her, "I am too afraid. He might beat me. He beats me too, so why should he believe me?"

She said, "That's true. We will tell Grandma and see what happens."

We had a snack and watched TV, and I went to sleep without crying, for the first time. I was happy, happy, happy at my aunt's and uncle's and cousins' house. That was all I knew. I didn't see my cousins kept in the house. They were happy and free about things.

The next day was Saturday, and we were going to Grandma's house. I hadn't seen her for a long time. We all ate and got dressed, and my uncle had a treat for us. He was taking us to a place called Coney Island. They said it was a fine place, with games, toys, food, candy, a beach, and lots and lots of rides.

We went off to Grandma's house. She had lots of food, and a lovely apartment with lots of pictures on the walls. She kissed me, gave me a real big hug, and told me I looked pretty.

I asked her if she knew where my mother was.

She said no.

I told her I was not happy, and I began to tell her my story.

She had tears as she said, "That's my son. I must talk to him about this."

I said, "No! He's going to hit me, and my stepmom will too. He is not going to believe you. My stepmom will make me afraid. She will wait till no one is around and hit me and punish me, every day."

I really felt I would get hurt if I told the whole story???

Wow! I miss all this, living with my stepmom. Why me? Why me? I asked myself. *I must take my mind off my stepmom. I have to block her out completely.*

Well, we were walking, laughing, and looking all around.

"Oh, look at that! What's that?"

"What a ride!"

They knew I had never been to Coney Island before. It was beautiful, with a big beach and people swimming. I could not swim at all, but everybody was having fun.

My aunt yelled, "Kids, choose a ride, and I'll go get tickets."

She did, and there were so many of them, just so we could ride and have fun. She gave me money to play any game I wanted.

Beautiful! Money for me to spend! I was laughing, riding, joking, happy, eating.

I found time to be with my aunt, and I told her, "I don't have fun like this. My stepmom takes me nowhere. My dad either. Only to school, the store, and home."

My aunt said, "That is really sad. We are going to help you, somehow. Don't worry. Be patient."

I said, "I hope so. I've waited so long for something like this."

She said, "Don't worry. We will have more time like this."

I smiled at her.

We were eating hot dogs, cotton candy, French fries, and ice cream, and drinking soda. Half the day went by.

I was hurting all over again. The next day was Sunday, and I was sad.

I don't want to go back over there, I said to myself.

I was getting my clothes ready to pack for when my dad picked me up. I was nervous, thinking I had to go back. I was crying. I wished I did not have to go back, but I knew I had to. Getting closer.

By the time I went upstairs, my dad was blowing the horn for me to come down. My heart was beating fast. I was nervous. I thought everything would turn black.

I kissed everyone, and I had tears in my eyes. My aunt walked me down to where he was in the car.

She said, "Come in for a while," and he said no.

My dad said, "You must go back home."

"I am not happy."

He said, "I'll take you back next weekend."

Then I got happy and said, "I want to see my mom. I want to know where she is. I asked Grandma, and she doesn't know where she lives."

We were almost home, and I was choked up. Then we were there.

As my dad locked the door to the car, he said, "Go up. I'll catch up."

I went up and knocked on the door, and my stepmom opened the door. She looked at me and questioned me about who I saw and what I did.

I told her, "I had so much fun, I didn't want to come back."

She said, "You live here with your dad. You must stay here."

My dad came up, and I went into the room that I shared with my step sister. I told her I didn't want to come back.

She said, "I believe you."

"Well, they know how I feel anyway."

My dad came in and told my stepmom I was not happy here.

She said, "That's because your family put that in her head."

My dad said, "Why is my daughter saying that? Why?"

My stepmom said. "You should never have taken her over there. We will have problems now."

After a while they forgot about it.

Then my stepmom said, "You will not be going all the time."

I just looked at her, upset, and said to myself, *That's what she thinks.*

I gave her a smart look and walked away.

The next day was school. At least I spent most of the day in school, better than being with my stepmom. She got me up early to go to the store, run an errand. I came back, walking, made the beds, and everybody left for school.

I was still there, the last one to go to school. I did my chores and errands, and was late getting to school, as always.

After being in school all day long, I saw the girls who picked on me. They told me some of them would beat me up. School was over, and guess what. I got beat.

I got home late, and that meant another beating. They would not believe I got beat up. As I got home, I was afraid.

I came in, and my stepmom said, "Get in here. You are late again. What's the excuse?"

I told her, "I got beat up. They kicked me and pulled my hair."

What did she care? I got a beating anyway, and from my dad.

I was so upset, I didn't want to eat as I was standing in front of the stove. That's how I ate, standing up, at all times, every day. Everybody else had a chair, and I had to stand up. I was hurt inside.

My dad didn't see everything that was going on. He came home from work, we all ate, and everything. He would never believe me at all.

After my dad hit me, I screamed and said, "I do not want to be here!"

I went in my room and cried myself to sleep.

The next day came, and I had to get up and buy the newspaper. I remembered my aunt's phone number that she gave me. I stole the newspaper and called her early in the morning.

She asked me, "What are you doing out in the street at six o'clock in the morning?"

I told her, "Buying a newspaper and going to the store. I have to do it."

She said, "I believe you. Does your dad know you are out there?"

"No," I said. "He leaves for work early in the morning."

She was upset, and very mad.

"Your stepmom should go herself instead of sending you. Something could happen to you."

"I know," I answered, "but I'm used to it."

"Well, I am going to call your dad at his job and tell him."

I hung up and went back home. Then I went to school. I was not happy anymore.

After school I went home, and my stepmom told me something, and I got smart with her. She hit me, pulled my hair, and kept hitting me. I went in my room.

My stepsister was invited out to a movie. I was upset, because I could not go. She left, and I had to clean, as always.

My stepsister was out for a while. She got anything she wanted – nice clothes, nice things – but I didn't. I always wore long dresses, white sneakers, and the same skirts all the time.

It was Friday already. My stepmom asked me something, and I backtalked her. Then she got mad and hit me.

She said, "You're going to be punished this time."

My stepsister and I had to put our knees on a lid on the floor – a lid from a big can with a hole in it. We had to put our knees on it, and it hurt.

My stepmom said, "They do that in Puerto Rico. That's how they get punished, for half an hour."

That was that. I did not want to get on them again.

My stepmom said, "Nobody goes anywhere this weekend because of bad behavior."

I was so upset that I thought, *Why? Why me? I've got to get out of here. I must call my aunt.*

I was hoping she would send me to the store, and I could call my aunt.

A while later my stepmom said, "Go to the store."

I got ready, went to the store, and kept the dime. I called my aunt, and she answered the phone.

I said, "Help me! Get me out of here! Find my mom, please!"

My aunt said, "I'll go call your dad today.'

"Please," I replied, "I don't want to be here!"

"Okay," she said. "Be good, so you don't get hit."

"I'll try," I told her.

It felt good, telling my aunt my problem.

Thank God – but suppose my stepmom finds out. I started thinking. My aunt is going to call my dad, and I am going to get a beating. Well, so what? Maybe they will get tired of me.

I really felt scared and worried. I went back home, and my stepmom said I took too long. I did not say anything.

She said, "Next time I'll send you with one of your stepsisters."

I got worried. It was the only time I could call my aunt, when I went to the store.

The next day it was the same old routine – the store, the newspaper – and I did not call my aunt.

I'll call her when something happens again, I thought.

I went to school and had a nice day. My favorite classes were music and English. I was not too great in math. I did not put my mind to it, because I had so many problems.

It was getting to be time for school to be over, and I was thinking, *Maybe I can go away for the whole summer. Wouldn't that be great? Wouldn't I be happy?*

My stepsister always acted like she had the most in the house. She was the smartest in the house. She was a smart girl, but she had her mom, and I didn't. I started lacking in school work also. Getting hit and no love at home – that made me a miserable kid.

Then school was over. Kids talked about having fun all summer long during vacation – except me. I didn't say anything. It was the month of June, and it was really warm out, almost summertime.

My aunt must get me out of here! She said she would. What's taking so long? Where's my mom? Maybe this summer something good will happen.

I was in my room, and I refused to talk to anybody. I was really upset about being there. The kids always watched me get beat, and I wondered what they thought of me.

I said, "One day this is going to stop. They won't watch me anymore."

I kept being smart.

My stepmom said, "Your dad will be home soon, so I can tell him."

He came home, my stepmom told him, and he hit me.

He said, "you like to get hit?"

I said, "No. I want to go to my aunt's house."

He looked at me and sent me to my room. Anyway, I cried louder and louder. I couldn't even eat supper, that's how hurt I was. I wasn't hungry and just took a bath and went to bed.

The next day I had to call my aunt again when my stepmom sent me to the store in the morning. I got up, and I did just that. I called her.

I asked her, "When are you going to help me get out from there?"

She said she had called my dad, but he was out on the road. He was a truck driver.

"I'll call him again. Don't worry. I told Grandma to try to get hold of your dad, once and for all."

She told me again to be good.

"I'll try."

I hung up. I did not want to stay out too long.

She'll know something if I take too long.

I hurried back, and when I got there, I had tears in my eyes. Just being there made me sick.

It was about nine o'clock, and my dad did not show up from work. My stepmom was so upset, it was not funny.

She said, "Where can he be?"

I was really happy that she was upset, worrying where my dad was. Anyway, it was time for us to go to sleep, and still he did not show up.

The next morning my dad still did not come home. I was happy. She had hurt me so much, and she was furious. Anyway, it was afternoon when my dad showed up.

My stepmom hollered and screamed, "Where were you all night long? Where?"

My dad smiled, and she screamed and threw something. He turned around and hit her. I was happy, laughing a little where nobody saw me.

My dad told her to stop, that he needed some sleep. Then he went to sleep.

My stepmom said, "You liked that, didn't you? I know you did."

I just went in my bedroom. I was happy. She always hit me, and I wondered how she felt getting hit.

That same day my dad got up, ate, took a bath, got dressed, and got ready to go out.

My stepmom hollered, "No, not again! You are not going out."

He said, "Yes, I am," and he did.

I thought, *I hope she doesn't take it out on me because of what my dad is doing.*

My dad did not come home that night either. He came home the next day.

She was crying. "Why are you staying out like this?"

"Hanging out with my friends," he said.

"Stay home with me," she told him.

I started thinking, *Maybe my aunt told my dad. He is upset about something. Maybe...oh, it's just all in my mind. I'll never leave here. I know I cannot live here forever. I must get big sometime.*

Well, I called my aunt and told her what's going on here. Did she talk to my dad?

I woke up, and my stepmother sent me to get the newspaper. I took it, kept the dime, and called her.

She told me hello and asked if I was good.

I said, "Yes. Did you call my dad?"

"Yes," she said, "I did. I really did. He said he'll check it out."

"He doesn't believe I'm being mistreated. He'll ask my stepmom."

"I don't believe he'll ask her."

I told my aunt that my dad and stepmom were fighting and arguing, and that he was staying out.

"Don't worry," my aunt said. "It'll be over soon."

I went back home.

I was twelve years old now, and it was my birthday on July first. Anyway, my aunt called my dad and said to bring me over for my birthday. They were having a big party for me.

My dad told my stepmom, and she did not seem happy about it. My dad told me to pack for the weekend, because there was going to be a birthday party for me.

Hooray! Hooray! I'm going! I'm going! I'll be so happy. I'm having a big party. Great!

My heart was beating fast.

The next day was Friday. I was ready, and nobody could say anything to me. I was waiting for my dad. He came, and it was time to go.

I was happy, and he said, "You are happy."

I said, "Yes. I'm going to my aunt's. I am happy."

I had nothing else on my mind but fun, being away from the house. We arrived, but my birthday wasn't until Saturday. I went into my aunt's house, and everybody was happy, especially me. I was so happy, I cried.

My aunt said, "I know how you feel. It's all right."

My dad looked at me like he was a little sad. At the same time I was really happy. There was something he knew, something he kept inside.

My dad sat down, watching TV, and my aunt made a big dinner. I did not see balloons or anything for my birthday.

Maybe I'll see it tomorrow, I thought.

My aunt made a lot of food. There was ice cream for dessert, and a little of everything. It was nice, and a lot of food was left over. That was fun.

Anyway, a truck came by with a ride on it, a small one. It had a bench on each level, and it went up and down, halfway sideways. Boy, that was fun. Everybody made a line, all the kids on the block, and I wanted to get on again, but I changed my mind.

My aunt yelled out the window, "Get on it again!"

"Maybe tomorrow," I said.

The line was too long.

We stayed out playing games, jumping rope, and skipping. The neighbors downstairs left the dog out, and we were playing with it. A man came around selling snow cones on a cart. We bought some. I liked cherry flavor. Time goes fast when you are having fun.

My uncle called us up to wash our hands to eat. Then we had baths, snacks, and a little TV before bedtime. My aunt and I had time to talk. I told her my dad was staying out, and that my stepmom and dad had been arguing and fighting.

"I am happy," she said. "Maybe they will leave each other."

"Yeah, yeah!" I said.

My aunt said, "Maybe. When we talked to your dad, he did not believe that your stepmom is mistreating you."

I put my head down. "How can I convince someone that I am getting hit? Only my grandma and aunt know about it, and my uncle. I need to prove it to my dad. I am so scared because of my stepmom."

Anyway, it was time to go to sleep.

My uncle came into the room and said, "We have a surprise for you tomorrow."

I smiled. I was laughing, inside me.

A surprise! I love this!

It was the most I ever got, the happiest I had ever been. I really did not get much of anything with my stepmom – nothing.

Anyway, I fell asleep and woke up in the morning. We had breakfast after we brushed our teeth, then watched cartoons, without doing chores, and no one was screaming at me. I was not going out to get the newspaper early in the morning. I was happy at my aunt's. I found love there. They treated me wonderful and gave me freedom. I did not feel so caged inside, locked in.

Anyway, we bathed and dressed pretty, then ate and got ready to leave for the birthday party.

As we drove, I asked, "Where are we going?"

"To Grandma's house."

I wanted to see my grandma. We arrived there, and they told me to go up first. I went in, and there were balloons everywhere. A big birthday cake was on the table, with lots of food. It was so pretty, I started crying.

My grandma kissed me. I loved my grandma so much – she did this for me!

My aunt, uncle, and cousins came up. They played records to dance. I didn't dance that well, as I never went dancing. Anyway, I was learning.

My grandma said, "We have a lot of people coming over later."

I said, "People who are friends of my family?"

I did not know all the family.

Then people started coming over. My grandma said, "This is my granddaughter, who was away from us."

They kissed me and treated me nice.

"Happy birthday! Happy birthday!" That was all I heard.

There were presents too. I looked at my grandma's bed, and it was full of presents.

I asked, "Whose is this?"

My grandma said, "Yours. Open them if you want, now or later."

I opened a couple. I got dresses, stockings, nice rings. It was nice. I wished the party would never end.

Anyway, people in the family danced, laughed, and joked. We had soda, chips, and so much food, it lasted till midnight.

I was falling asleep, and my grandma said, "You're spending the night here."

"I am?"

I undressed, put on pajamas, and went to sleep.

When I woke up in the morning, I opened my eyes, and I was still at Grandma's, not at my stepmom's house. I started to help cleaning some leftovers that were not done.

My grandma asked, "What's for breakfast?"

"I am not used to anyone asking me what I want."

I asked for Cheerios, my favorite, and that was what she gave me – and juice. I was happy.

She said, "You leave tomorrow. I am going to ask your dad if you can stay with me for good."

I looked at her, my eyes and mouth wide open.

My grandma said, "It'll take time to convince your father. We will do it, unless your stepmom, does something, we can get you for real."

I took a long stretch with my arms.

Soon I'll be free, I thought, *from my stepmom. I guess I'll hold on until everything is all over.*

My grandma and I cleaned and ate. I asked her if we could go to my aunt's house. She said yes, just like that.

"Oh, boy!" I said. "I am having fun."

My grandma said, "We are having a surprise before you go home."

Another surprise? I wonder what it is.

We left and caught the bus to my aunts house. It was out that far. We arrived, and I was still wondering what the surprise was.

My uncle said, "Everybody get in the car."

"Where are we going?" my aunt asked.

"Coney Island."

I was so happy, I said, "I don't want to go home with my stepmom again."

They looked at me and told me, "Do not worry. Be patience. You'll be all right. Be good, and do nothing, so she won't hit you. That means don't talk back to her. Don't make her upset, and she won't hit you. Try hard."

"I'll try hard," I said.

My aunt said, "Try harder."

Anyway, we left and went to Coney Island. We couldn't stay long, because I had to be back so my dad could pick me up.

Well, I was at my aunt's house, waiting for my dad. An hour went by, then two, then three. My dad was late. Finally he arrived, and I got sad.

My aunt said, "Remember what I told you."

"I'll try," I said, and we left.

My dad asked if I had a lot of fun. I was quiet. I did not say anything all the way home. We got there, and it was dark already.

I took a bath for bed, and I was still sad, because there I was again. I forced myself to sleep. Anyway, it was a nice weekend.

It was back to school again, and I had to do chores, as always. I was upset again, but I had to be careful that my stepmom would not hit me or take anything out on me. After chores I was really happy to be in school all day long, until three o'clock.

When school was over, I was back home.

My stepmom said, "We'll start going to church again. Catholic."

That was nice. I would get to be out of the house for a little while. We went.

Anyway, my dad was late from work again, and my stepmom was upset, waiting for him to come home. In fact, she was very upset.

We did our chores, and it was time to go to sleep.

My dad came home late, and from my bedroom I heard the screaming and breaking things. I stayed in my room, real happy, with a smile. My stepsister noticed my expression on my face, that I was not upset. She was crying. I was not.

The next day came, and my dad was not speaking to my stepmom. He got dressed for work, and he left.

Then my stepsister told on me!

She said to me, "You laughed and smiled."

My stepmom said, "She likes that – us arguing."

She hit me. I talked back to her and everything. Then I went in my room, got ready for school, and did my chores.

That day after school I wrote a letter – I just had to – about myself. I wrote:

I do not want to be here anymore.

I believe I wrote:

I want to kill myself and jump off
the Brooklyn Bridge if somebody
doesn't get me out of here.

I clearly remember *Brooklyn Bridge* coming over me.

Now, my mistake was that my stepsister saw me when I was writing. She saw where I hid it. I thought I hid it, but I guess not.

I went to the store, and when I came back, my stepmom, had the letter in her hand.

She said, "Yeah, you do not want to be here, and you want to kill yourself."

She gave me a big beating for that.

My stepsister told me she found it and gave it to her.

I didn't want to be here anymore, but I had to be there whether I wanted to or not. I just had to wait.

Time went by, and it was the same old thing. My dad stayed out more than ever. There was the same arguing, chores, and house. I wasn't leaving for the weekend.

One day my stepmom picked the right day to show my dad that

letter. She showed it to him, and my dad was so upset that he picked me up and threw me on the floor. I landed next to the heater, the radiator, on my back.

I was screaming, "I can't take her anymore! If it isn't her beating me, it's you beating me! How much more can I take?"

My dad yelled, "What have I done wrong? I always work, put food on the table. You don't want to be here? Why? Why?"

All I did was cry, just cry. I did not eat. Every time I tried to eat, I felt like throwing up. I was so nervous, I just couldn't eat. I was too upset to eat. My stepmom told my dad I couldn't eat.

"What's wrong?" my dad asked me.

I wouldn't answer him.

He said, "I don't like to hit you. I get upset with you."

I didn't say anything. I just went in my room. He realized something was wrong with me.

Well, that was over. Things were a little calm, but the problems always remained, the same old things.

One day the neighbor upstairs came down to talk to my stepmom.

I opened the door, and she asked me, "Did you read the paper?"

I said, "No. Why?"

She said, "Your mother is looking for you."

My eyes popped wide open. "What?"

"It's in the Spanish newspaper," the neighbor said. "It's called *El Edario*. Your mom, is looking for her daughter, and her father, whom she hasn't seen for many years. She left her name and address and telephone to please contact her. She lives in the Bronx, New York."

Then my stepmom walked in. She went in her bedroom. I was in shock.

The neighbor asked her, "Did you read the newspaper? They are looking for your stepdaughter."

She said, "Come here," where I couldn't hear.

I went in my room, hoping she would send me to the store, so I could call me aunt and tell her the good news. After a while she did send me, and that was my chance to call my aunt.

I knew this was it. I knew I was getting close to leaving that house and my stepmom.

I went to the store and kept the dime to make the phone call. I dialed her number, and my aunt answered the phone.

I said, "Hi. It's me. Go buy the newspaper. My mom is looking for me."

"How do you know?" she asked.

"The neighbor came and told me."

She said, "I'll buy the newspaper, and I'll let you know if that's your mom or what."

"Okay," I said. "Please hurry. I'll try to call back. Call my mom. Talk to you later."

In the meantime I went home. My stepmom and the lady upstairs were still talking about me and my dad. After a while she left, and my stepmom looked at me, but she did not say much.

After a while she said, "Your mom is looking for you."

She said nothing else, because I was so happy, nobody could tell me anything. I could have screamed and jumped high, except I couldn't. My stepmom wouldn't like that – me being happy.

Anyway, I was waiting for my dad, for him to hear the good news.

I don't know how he is going to take this, I thought.

After a while my dad came home, and my stepmom told him about the newspaper. "Her mom is looking for your daughter."

He hit the ceiling. "What? She's not going anywhere! She's staying with me!"

My stepmom came out to the kitchen. She smiled at me. In other words, I wasn't going anywhere.

I didn't pay it any mind, because I had called my aunt.

They are going to help me out for sure.

I went in my room anyway. I did my chores, bathed, and was ready for bed. I just had to wait till the next day to call my aunt and find out what happened.

My dad was calling me, and I wondered what he was going to say. I went out to the kitchen.

He said, "I know you know your mom is looking for you after all these years, but you are staying here with me now. Soon as we find out some more information about where she lives, I'll take you, only for a visit, and that is it."

"Okay," I said.

I'm going to tell my mom everything that is happening to me, I thought.

So I went in to go to sleep.

The next morning I got up, dressed, and was ready to get the newspaper.

My stepmom called me and said, "Go to the store and get the newspaper."

"Okay," I said.

I went to the store, took the newspaper, and called my aunt.

When she answered, I said, "It's me. What happened about my mom?"

"I called the number in the newspaper," she told me, "and guess what. It's your mom."

I started crying and asked, "Did you tell her everything about what's going on with me?"

She said, "She wants to see you. She started crying and said, 'I want to see my daughter. Her dad took her from me. I want to see her. If I hadn't called the newspaper, I would never have seen her again.'"

My aunt gave her the phone number where he worked.

I said, "Well, I am happy. I'm staying with my dad, and I am only going to visit my mom. That's it."

My aunt replied, "We'll see. You've been through enough. Somebody should do something now."

I told my aunt to tell my mom I would visit her, my dad said, but I couldn't stay with her. Anyway, I have to hang up, because I'm taking a little too long on the phone. My stepmom will wonder what's keeping me. I'll call you and keep in touch."

I hung up.

School is almost over now, I thought. *I wonder if I can leave my stepmom's house for good.*

I went back home, and my stepmom asked what took me so long. I told her I was walking slow.

"Next time," she said, "hurry up, 'cause I time you. It shouldn't take you so long where I sent you."

"Okay," I said.

I went to school and was happy to be there. As always, I would rather be in school than be home with my stepmom.

At three o'clock I went home, and my stepmom said, "Your dad came home for lunch. He wants you to go to your aunt's this weekend."

"Good," I said.

I went in my room, and I was really happy. I could do any chore she gave me. That's how happy I was. I was wondering if my mom called my dad. I was anxious to find out what was going on.

Well, I had to wait regardless. I was anxious for the weekend to go to my aunt's.

Then I thought of something. *When I go to my aunt's, I can call my mom for real! Everything is going to be real. My own mom. My real mom!*

Anyway, I just couldn't wait. It was Wednesday already. I had two more days till Friday.

Thursday came, and I went to school. Those girls picked on me again, but this time I decided that if they hit me, I was going to hit them back. I knew I couldn't beat them all, but at least one of them, and that would make me happy.

After school the girls picked at me, calling me names, and I just kept going. They did not hit me, and I was glad for that.

I went home, and my stepmom said, "You've got a lot of chores before you leave tomorrow."

I had to wash clothes, at the laundry place.

"Okay, I will," I said.

I started doing chores, and she said, "You must do all your chores for Friday, or you can't go."

I got sad – but I always did get sad. *I must do my chores after school, and I can leave.*

My dad got off work early, a surprise, because he never did that. He hung around the house, watching things. It looked like he was watching television, and my stepmom treated me nice. I wondered why – and then I figured it out.

My dad is here. That's why she's treating me nice. If only my dad knew everything....

Well, he just did not believe us at all.

My dad came to me and said, "Make sure you pack your things to go to your aunt's house tomorrow."

I said, "Yes, fine."

He told my stepmom, "I am going out."

"Don't stay out," she said. "Are you coming home early?"

"Yes," he replied.

Oh, no! I thought. *I hope he comes back to take me to my aunt's house. I hope he doesn't drink too much. If he does, he'll forget to come back.*

I did my chores and tried to eat supper. That was my problem. I couldn't eat a lot. I didn't want to eat.

Then it was bath time, and bedtime. I was watching the time, to make sure it was not too late. My dad had not come home yet.

We went to sleep, and I didn't hear my dad come in. It was late when he came home, and they started arguing again. They were really going at it.

I hope my dad still takes me to my aunt's house, I thought.

I went to sleep again and woke up to go to school. I did my chores and did not call my aunt.

I'll see her today after school. At least I hope I'll go to her house.

I was so anxious, I couldn't think in school. All I had on my mind was my aunt – and my mom. When school was over, I ran all the way home.

When I got there my stepmom said, "Do your chores. Your father is not here yet."

So I changed clothes. I had my clothes packed already and was doing my chores, waiting for my dad to come in.

After a while he came, and he asked me, "Are you ready?"

I said, "Yes, but I didn't finish my chores."

My stepmom said, "Finish your chores."

"No, come on," my dad said. "Don't worry about it."

I left, and I was happy.

On the way over to my aunt's house, my dad said, "I love you. Have fun."

He turned on the radio in the car, and we listened to Spanish music until we arrived there.

We went up, and my uncle asked my dad, "Did you hear the news? Your ex-wife's been looking for your daughter, in the newspaper."

"Yes, I know," my dad replied. "She called me on the job. She wants to see our daughter."

I was really happy, overjoyed.

I'm going to see my mom! I thought. *Suppose my mom doesn't love me. She has to love me all over again. I was so small when my dad took me away....*

I was thinking about how my mom felt about me.

Will she take me and raise me and not punish me?

My mom had another husband.

Maybe he won't like me.

All these things were running through my mind.

Do I have more brothers and sisters?

I got really nervous.

What's going to happen to me? Who is really going to take me in and raise me? Who is going to love me? Who is going to take me out so I can have fun. When will this all be over?

My aunt said, "You can call your mom if you like."

I looked at her. "Me call? What should I say?"

"Just say who you are," my aunt said. "Tell her about school, and about your stepmom, and about your dad."

"I'm afraid," I told her. "Suppose she doesn't like me."

"Call her," she insisted.

My heart was beating fast, I was so nervous – but I called.

A lady answered the phone. It was my mom!

I said, "It's me."

"You are a big girl now," my mom said, and she asked how I was doing. She asked me about school.

I said, "It's fine." Then I asked, "Why didn't you come and get me, see me, help me? you know, my stepmom did so much to me."

"I know," she replied. "I am sorry. I was afraid to. Your father threatened me, that I was never to take you."

She said I had two brothers and a sister. Boy, was I happy.

"I spoke to your father," she said. "He will bring you over to visit me next weekend."

"All right," I said. "You sure my dad will take me to see you?"

"Yes. He has the address and everything."

"Okay," I said.

"I'll see you next week," my mom said.

"All right," I replied. "Bye."

"Bye."

My aunt asked, "Was your conversation okay? How did it go?"

"Fine for now," I said.

"Change clothes," my aunt told me, "and go out and play."

I jumped up and said, "Okay!"

My cousins were good to me. They loved me like we were brothers and sisters, like a real family.

My dad said he was leaving.

I said good-bye, then went outside and jumped rope, my favorite thing. They were learning how to jump "double Dutch." It looked like fun, and I tried it, but I messed up. I tried again and again until I got the hang of it. I wanted to jump all night long.

I never did things like this when I lived with my stepmom. I never got to do anything but clean house and do chores. I never learned how to cook with her, but my stepsister learned how to do everything.

I was happy to be with my aunt. She was teaching me to do my hair. I didn't know how to comb it and put it in a ponytail.

She said, "There's more to life than that. Everybody must learn how to do everything in life."

I just stared at her, then asked, "Why does my stepmom do what she does to me?"

"Nobody knows what's going on," she replied. "She doesn't love you, like your real mother or me or your grandma."

Then we went back to my aunt's house and undressed. It was time to go to sleep, and we all did.

We all bathed and changed and went to the party, and when it was over, we went back to my aunt's, bathed, and went to sleep.

The next day was Sunday. That meant I had to go back to my stepmom's house. I was a little sad when we went to sleep.

We woke up and watched cartoons and the "Little Rascals." I love them. They made me laugh. Time was going fast. My dad would be here soon.

I got dressed, packed my clothes, and said to myself, *I wish I lived here and never had to leave.*

I had to wait for my dad to pick me up. He came, and I said good-bye to everybody, then left.

"Nice curls," my dad said.

I said, "My aunt took me to the beauty shop."

"That's nice. You look pretty."

"When am I going to my aunt's again?" I asked.

"Next weekend you are going to meet your mom for the weekend."

That made me happy.

Anyway, we got to my stepmom's house, and everything was still the same there.

My stepmom said, "Don't forget your chores."

I hated chores so much. Every day it was all I did. She said tomorrow I was going to iron.

"I will teach you how," she told me.

The next day, Monday, after school she was teaching me how to iron. I tried it, and I didn't do it right. I didn't want to do it. She told me I was doing it all sloppy, but I didn't care. All I wanted to do was leave there, that's all, for someone to take me away from all this.

I thought, *One day I want to tell the whole world about my stepmom.*

I finished the ironing, took a bath, and it was the same old routine. I was sick of everything. I hated myself when I was at my stepmom's house. I hated everything there. That was how I felt. Nobody loved me or wanted me there. They only wanted me to do chores and clean. I was always upset.

The week went by, and I was doing the same old thing. It was Friday, and I was going to meet my mom for the first time.

After school I bathed, changed, and dressed up to meet my mom. My dad got off work and had supper, and after a while we left to go to the Bronx. The drive seemed a little longer.

We got there, and it was a long climb to the fourth floor. We knocked, and a man answered the door. It was my mom's husband. We walked in, and said hello. There was my sister, my brother, and my step brother. They introduced everybody.

My mom came to me, gave me a big hug, and took me to her bedroom. My dad stayed talking to my mom's husband.

My mom asked me all kinds of questions. She told me a little about her and my dad, and she asked me about my stepmom.

I told her I did not want to live there anymore.

She began explaining to me what really happened to me, how my dad wanted me, and my grandma too. I was hearing different stories now.

One thing I noticed when she hugged me again. *How come I don't feel like I love her?*

I kept talking, and she started brushing my hair. I had long hair.

My dad called me out, and he said, "You're spending the weekend. I'll be back for you on Sunday."

I kissed him, and after he left, I felt like a stranger there. I felt different there.

They turned on the TV, and she made food for me, all kinds of things to eat, soda and all. Then my mom started talking about how my dad did her wrong, and my other aunt would talk mean to her. Nobody liked her, she told me.

I was feeling sad as we went out walking around. I told her how my stepmom treated me, and she felt awfully bad.

"I'm sorry," she said. "I can picture you being so unhappy."

I asked, "Does that mean that I am leaving my stepmom's house?"

She said, "You can visit us anytime you like. I don't know if I can take you just like that. It'll be a problem. We would have to go to court. I'm still afraid of going to court, because he had you so long, all this time. I'm afraid I'll lose in court."

She said, "That's what happened in the beginning. Your dad would have hit me, and I was too afraid."

We talked more and more about my dad.

"I feel a lot for my dad," I told her.

She said, "Enjoy yourself while you are, and I'll talk to your dad about this. I don't think he'll let you go just like that."

I forgot about it for a while. We ate, watched more TV, went to the park, and came home. I was excited. My mom treated me real nice, and my brother and sister played games with me. We played "Superman."

Anyway, the weekend was over.

My mom said, "Be good."

When my dad knocked on the door, he said, "Let's go."

My mom said, "Call me again. Bring her back when she wants."

We went back toward my stepmom's house, and I started getting sad again. I just hated to go back there.

When we got there, my stepmom asked, "Did you meet your mom?"

"Yes," I said. "I was happy."

My stepmom sent me to the store, and I called my aunt. I told her I had met my mom.

"She was nice and everything. Now I'm back at my stepmom's house."

She said, "Your grandma is going to talk to your dad about letting you stay with her. There's a good chance of it."

"I hope so," I said. "My mom said my dad told her I can't live with her, only visit."

I went back home, to my stepmom's, and my dad said, "You will not visit anyone for a while."

I was heartbroken.

"Why?" I asked.

"Just for a while."

I called my aunt to do something real fast. I was fourteen now, and it was my birthday. School was over in June, and my birthday was in July, and I had not visited anyone since June, a month later.

One day someone knocked on the door real hard. It was my aunt. She kept knocking real hard.

She told my stepmom, "Let me in!"

My stepmom said no.

"Give us her for the weekend. School is over, and her dad promised to bring her," my aunt said. "It's your fault she can't come to visit us anymore."

My stepmom, said, "Get away from the door. I am not going to open it. Wait till her dad gets off work."

My aunt left, but not before giving the door a good kick. She came back after my dad got off, and my dad hollered, and my aunt did too.

My dad said, "Now you won't see her at all."

My aunt left, and now I felt it was all over for me.

I'll never see them again!

It was August, and I had not seen them. I was sad. I stop calling my aunt. I felt there was no use. I was never leaving my stepmom's house.

It was chores as always, but now my stepmom said we were allowed to sit on the steps for an hour. That was it. I was really sad.

My dad pulled up in his car, and he looked at me and said hello.

"When are you taking me to my aunt's house?" I asked.

"Soon," he said.

I went upstairs, very sad. My dad ate and left.

I told my stepsister I wanted to leave here, that I could not take it anymore. Then she told my stepmom.

My stepmom screamed, "Yeah! She wants to leave."

She hit me and gave me a beating. "I am telling your dad!"

"Tell him!" I said. "I want to leave."

After a while my dad came, and the first thing my stepmom said was, "Your daughter wants to leave here. That's from you taking her to your family's house. She wants to leave now!"

My dad said, "So you want to leave here," and he hit me. "You want to leave?"

"Yes!" I responded. "I am not happy here."

"You will be sorry if you leave here," my dad said.

I went to my room, screaming and crying. I did not want to eat at all. I didn't want to do anything.

The next day I called my aunt and told her, "I will kill myself if no one comes to get me out of here!"

"I'll call your dad and tell him what's going on," she said.

"Good-bye," I said, and hung up.

I went back to the house, got ready for school, and went, very upset. I was being bad in school. I didn't care anymore.

I came home from school, and my dad said, "You will leave here soon."

That was all he said. I went to my room, as always, and it was the same old thing.

I thought of taking off. I was too afraid to do that. I was going to have to do it to leave though.

My stepmom always treated me like things were the same. I started not talking to anyone in the house. Maybe they would understand that I did not want to be there anymore.

My dad stopped taking me to visit my family, and as always, things stayed the same.

How can I get through to these people here?

I was sick of being there. They did not love me, and it hurt to feel like that every single day.

I cleaned and did chores, and it was August, my stepsister's birthday. She went out.

Lucky for her, I thought to myself. *One day I will leave.*

It was all I had on my mind to do.

Soon school started, and I was still at my stepmom's house. I broke out in chickenpox, and everybody got chickenpox. Everybody was itching and itching. My stepmom gave us medicine for it. I couldn't wait till that was over.

I still had eating problems, because I was so nervous. I tried to eat, but I felt like I had to throw up every time I ate. My stepmom knew it too. She would watch me as I forced myself to eat, always standing up by the stove, though sometimes I got to sit down to eat. I was getting really skinny.

That's how hurt I was. Every single day I was nervous, so one day my dad was talking to my stepmom about me.

My stepmom said, "She doesn't want to eat. She's doing it on purpose."

I wasn't. It was real. I just couldn't eat anyway.

They kept talking, and my stepmom asked me to do something. I got smart with her.

My dad said, "You're getting smart. You want to leave?"

"Yes!" I said.

"Well, if you want to leave here, I will never be your dad again."

I cried and cried.

"Fine," I said. "I just want to leave. I am not happy here."

"My dad said, "Did you hear me?"

"Yes," I said.

His eyes got real big, he was so angry, and he stared at me so hard, I thought he was going to go off again.

He said, "You will leave."

That's all he said. He walked out of the room. I wondered if he would hit me some more.

Later on I was thinking to myself, *Will he hit me again when he thinks about me leaving? He might hit me again. I hope not. My dad doesn't understand what I'm going through here. One day he will learn the truth about everything. I know my stepmom will never tell him the truth about the things she's done to me. Maybe not now, but one day she will realize what she did to me.*

I was in my room, and I did not want to come out. I knew what everyone must be thinking about me.

I am being treated badly here. I really am. I am not happy. My stepmom doesn't show me a nice time or take me to the movies, swimming, skating, bowling. The family doesn't do things together – but me, I am so unhappy, that's all I know.

Who would want to live like this? I wouldn't want anyone to have to live like this, miserable and unhappy. It's not good for anyone to live like this. It's terrible. I do not want to grow up like this. I don't believe I will be normal. I don't believe I can be happy as I get older. I would hate everyone. My feelings will never be corrected if I don't leave here.

I must leave. Oh, God, I want to be happy, like my aunt and uncle. They live happy. They go out. My cousins are happy. Why me? Why me?

My mom will help me, but I don't want to get my mom in trouble because of my problems. It's not her fault. She didn't know what I had been going through all these years. I never even knew my mom until now. She seems so nice. Will she do anything now to help me?

If it wasn't for that ad she put in the newspaper, she would never have found me. Thank God she did. I thank God for the lady upstairs. I would never have known. I am so glad there are good people in this world. They're not all like my stepmom.

Well, I'm going to try to get some sleep. I am not eating, and I don't want to get hit. No way, no more. I must be good until it's all over. I must hang in there and go along with whatever goes on here until someone or somebody takes me out of here.

I know I am leaving now for sure, because of what my dad told me. I know my dad was very angry at me because I want to leave. What does he know about me? He's always working and doesn't have time for me. If I tell him anything, she will really hit me. I am so afraid of that.

I also know that one day I'll be able to share this with everybody, tell the truth about my stepmom. If my father had never taken me from my mom, none of this would ever have happen to me. I would have been happy with my mom. I guess it was just not meant to be. I wouldn't be going through what I am going through.

One day my father will know the truth about me, and he will be so hurt. He will never believe me or anybody, not his own family, not even his mother. I guess he thinks everybody is making this up – unless he really does believe it and doesn't know how to face it. I know he must think about it and be afraid to admit it.

I have wondered over and over again why he can't believe it, his own daughter. Is it he is afraid of something? I don't understand why things have to be like they are. I know that I just can't keep going on like this. Nobody, but nobody, should live like this, certainly not any kid. It's sad.

I said to myself, One day I will tell my own kids, when I get big, that I will never do this to them. I want them to be happy, like any other kids, like my cousins. They are happy. They go out, they speak about their problems. Now that is beautiful. One day soon I'll be able to do the same.

I took a bath, and it was time to go to sleep, with school in the morning, thank God. Sometimes I wished there was school seven days a week, anything not to be with my stepmom.

One day I'll be free from all this. I'll go to freedom, happiness, not being nervous anymore, dressing nice in new shoes, coats, and my hair combed nice, with lots of other things I do not do now.

I thought, I hope I will not be mean because of the things my stepmom did, and also my dad hitting me, all because of what my stepmom would tell him.

I went to the kitchen, but nobody said anything to me, just looked at me as if I was a troublemaker. I wasn't a troublemaker. They saw what happened to me. They got hit but not like me, and they saw the way I was treated.

My day cannot come fast enough. What can I do, just look sad until they get tired of me? I am afraid to tell the police.

It was time to go to sleep. I had pain in my arm from being hit. I did not say anything. I felt it would start something if I said I was hurting from being hit.

The next day, as usual, there was school, chores, and after school my stepmom said my dad had to talk to me.

I wonder what it is. My mom? My aunt? Am I leaving after all. Or did my dad change his mind, and now I have to stay here?

I couldn't wait to hear what he was going to say.

It was getting late, and he did not show up yet. I was getting ready for bed when he finally came home, so I waited and said nothing. After a while he called me, and I went out into the kitchen.

He told me, "Sit down."

I did, and he said, "You are leaving here – but remember, I won't be your dad anymore."

I had tears in my eyes. They started running down my face.

"You are going to live with your grandma," he said.

My eyes got really big.

"Grandma!" I said, very happy, and I could not stop crying.

"When school is over, you can go for good. Is that what you want?"

"Yes!"

"Are you sure?" he asked me.

"Yes."

"Okay, then everything's settled. That's where you live."

I went in my bedroom and cried and cried. I felt sad for my dad though, and I was also crying because I was leaving him. Then I fell asleep.

The next day after school my stepmom looked at me and said, "You will be leaving soon, but you still do your chores until you leave."

"Okay," I said.

I was very happy, knowing it was almost over – no more beatings, no more getting up so early in the morning to go to the store and buy the newspaper when it was still dark. I was overjoyed. I would do anybody's chores. I would clean more than ever.

My step sister wasn't too happy. They knew I would be fine where I was going, with no more beatings and especially no more chores. I was really happy.

Time went by. One more week, and school would be over.

Then one day my stepmom told me, "Start packing your things. Whatever you don't need, throw it away. Just leave out the few things you will use."

She told me it was my job to make sure my clothes were clean.

I said, "All right, I will."

I started cleaning and everything, throwing things out so my stepmom wouldn't complain to my dad about anything. I did not want to upset her in any way, so she would not hit me for anything. Deep down inside I did not want to do it, but I just had to, or else I knew what would happen to me.

I was good, the best I could be. I did my chores, and I ate my supper, but there I had a problem. I was always upset, so it was really hard for me, but I would eat and throw away some food when she was not looking. I felt like I had to throw up my food, I got so sick to my stomach. I was too nervous and too upset.

I was always skinny. I don't believe I ever gained any weight, because I was always the same, always wearing the same long dresses and skirts and sneakers. That was all I wore, with pleats in them, especially the skirts.

I threw out a lot of things. My family would buy me more clothes and shoes and things. I really wanted to throw everything out. I did not want to have to take all those memories with me.

My stepmom was treating me good. I wondered why. I would not change my mind about leaving. I would never change my mind about that, but she treated me nice every single day, and even my stepsister and stepbrother did too.

In the couple of days I had remaining, I was somewhat happy, only because I knew it was over, but I had to be patient and wait.

My stepsister said, "Don't forget to visit us, okay?"

I just looked at her.

Are they kidding? Don't they know I am not coming back, not even to visit?

I was too hurt to come back.

Anyway, my one stepsister started acting real nice to me, but I was not changing my mind, that was for sure. Nothing or nobody would cause me to do that. I was too anxious to be happy, instead of always sad and hurt. It was horrible to feel that way every single day.

School kept me going, and in a couple of days it was over. My things were packed, and I was waiting for my dad to leave.

I said to myself, *What time is my dad coming? It's getting late.*

It was late – too late.

Finally my stepmom said, "Go to sleep."

I was upset, really upset. "Where is my dad?"

I figured he must have stepped out again. We all went to sleep, and my dad showed up the next day.

He told me he was sorry, "But I need sleep. Wait till tomorrow."

Well, I could wait one more day. It wouldn't hurt. I hoped he would take me and not forget or change his mind. I went to sleep.

We were not going to leave until the afternoon, and I was waiting patiently. Finally the time came, and everybody said good-bye, even my stepmom. My heart was going fast from being so nervous, but I was really happy. I could have screamed or cried, but I held myself back.

So, we were on our way to Grandma's house, and I was really happy. My dad did not say too much. He turned on the radio.

Then he said, "You are leaving now, you know that."

I said, "Yes, it's over."

I was really happy and couldn't wait to get to my grandma's house.

Finally we were there, and I felt one big wave of relief. We knocked on her door, and she opened it. I gave her a big hug.

My grandma! Wow! Free! Free! Free!

It was all I could think of, doing everything with love and happiness.

My grandma and my dad and I sat down together.

My dad said, "Take good care of her. I will see that she gets what she needs, and if she does not listen or misbehaves, give me a call. I'll be here right away."

My father stayed a few minutes, watching TV, and then my grandma showed me my own room, with a dresser. It was wonderful – no more hassles from my stepmom; no beatings from her and my dad at the same time.

My father yelled, "I am leaving!"

I went and kissed him on the cheek. I felt a little sad knowing he was leaving and I wouldn't be staying with him anymore. It was funny how I felt that way. I wanted to leave my stepmom, not him.

Well, I would get to see him sometimes. I could call, and I would still be happy.

I still believe, I thought, *one day he will learn the truth. Whether he believes me or not, he will have to live with that.*

He left, and I shut the door. Then my grandma gave me something to eat. She asked me what I would like to do, visit my aunt, go to a park or a movie, or visit one of my friends.

I told her I wanted to visit my aunt.

She said, "Fine. Let's go."

Just like that! She asked me what I would like to do, and she did it. My stepmom did not do things like that with me.

We went to my aunt's house. My grandma and my aunt and I sat at her kitchen table and talked about the past, when I was small, and about my mom.

They were young in Puerto Rico. I was leaving everything, and I did not know about them. Then my grandma made something clear to me.

She said, "About your stepmom. One day she will pay for everything she did to you," said and added, "There's a God up there in heaven." He knows everything.

She told me, "Go play. Enjoy yourself."

I just felt so free, I did not know how to act. I listened. I took baths. I helped clean. I changed to a new school, and as days went by, I started calling my grandma "Mommy," not Grandma. She was like my mom.

I didn't hear from my mom for a while, and then one day she called. She wanted to know how I was doing. I told her I was living with my grandma, and now I was really happy.

She said, "They will tell you things about me, and it won't be the truth."

I was confused then. I asked why.

She said, "When you get older, you will understand the whole story, why I couldn't help you."

I said to myself, *There is more to this than I thought.*

"I'll call you," she said. "Come visit me."

I asked, "Why don't you visit me here?"

"I can't," she said. "One day I'll tell you why, but not on the phone."

So I said good-bye.

Now I was in junior high school. I was learning all kinds of things, like about boyfriends. My friends had boyfriends and said one day I would have one too.

I asked my grandma about boyfriends, and she said, "It's nice to have a friend, but you're too young for a boyfriend."

I stayed with my Grandma for a few years. I was going to high school, growing and learning. I remained with my grandmother and family and grew to learn to be happy. Doing different things with family.

So much love to give I knew it would be all different now that it is over.

About the Author

I stay at home and I work from home. I also enjoy being with my children and grandchildren. When I am not writing I like to read other books. I like to read books on discoveries and books about god. I like to listen to christian music as well. I have interest in volunteering for the community and serving those in need in the church. I do attend church. I like to reach out to others and children. I remained with my grandmother and family. Doing things differently now and so much love to give. As a young child I wanted to write my story and my story doesn't stop here. This is my testimony. I dedicate this book to my children and family, with all my love!

Printed in the United States
by Bookmasters

Printed in the United States
By Bookmasters